Omveien

A Solo Female Wanderer Hiking Guide

Omveien, A Solo Female Wanderer Hiking Guide. ISBN 978-1-961878-33-4. Copyright 2025 by Sarah Rowe. For more information about this hiking guide and others, email hi@solofemalewanderer.com

A portion of the proceeds from the sale of this guide are donated to DNT to support their work maintaining the trail system and cabins.

Maps are from Kartverket under its Creative Commons license.

Introduction

Omveien in Norwegian means "the detour", and that's an appropriate description for this hike.

You could drive from Lillehammer to the end of the Sognefjord in 3 hours, or you could spend 16 days wandering through some of Norway's most spectacular landscapes. Start in the gently rolling mountains and old farms in Langsua, then climb into Jotunheimen's peaks. End the hike along the Sognefjord and dip your hand into the cold fjord water. Take detours along the way to Galdhøpiggen, Norway's highest peak, or Besseggen.

The most efficient route? No. An adventure well worth having? Yes.

Table of Contents

Route

Day	From	To	Distance (km)	
1	Storlondammen	Skjellbreidhytta	14.2	
2	Skjellbreidhytta	Kittilbua	11.7	
3	Kittilbua	Vestfjellhytta	17.2	
4	Vestfjellhytta	Liomseter	12.8	
5	Liomseter	Storkvolvbua	14.5	
6	Storkvolvbua	Storhøliseter	12.7	
7	Storhøliseter	Oskampen	13.2	
8	Oskampen	Sikkilsdalsseter	11.1	
9	Sikkilsdalsseter	Gjendesheim	16.3	
10	Gjendesheim	Glitterheim	21.8	
11	Glitterheim	Spiterstueln (Glittertinden)	17.2	
12	Spiterstulen	Leirvassbu	15.9	
13	Leirvassbu	Olavsbu	10.6	
14	Olavsbu	Skogadalsbøen	18.2	
15	Skogadalsbøen	Vettismorki	10.2	
16	Vettismorki	Øvre Årdal	2.7	

Up (meters)	Down (meters)	Time	Level
322	49	4 hours	Moderate
316	415	4 hours	Moderate
571	436	6.5 hours	Challenging
470	442	4 hours	Moderate
552	276	5 hours	Moderate
304	531	4 hours	Moderate
366	161	4 hours	Moderate
547	730	5 hours	Moderate
906	904	8 hours	Challenging
969	582	8 hours	Challenging
1,378	1,672	8 hours	Challenging
458	147	5 hours	Challenging
363	327	3.5 hours	Challenging
232	839	6 hours	Moderate
551	700	5 hours	Challenging
77	464	4 hours	Moderate

Storlondammen to Skjellbreidhytta

| 14.2 km | 322 meters | 49 meters | 4 hours |
| 8.8 miles | 1,056 feet | 160 feet | Moderate |

The start of the trail, Storlondammen, sits along the side of county road 250, which goes in between Lillehammer and Dokka. The recommended track is to just follow the road, Svartdalsvegen, between Storlondammen and Skjellbreidhytta. There are several wet and marshy areas in the area, and the road avoids those. The road is in use by the private cabins and farmers along the area, but isn't busy.

After a couple kilometers following the road, the path goes through Vismundsetra, a farm with a view of the river. After you walk through Vismundsetra, you'll go through the forest for 6km before you see Vismundvatnet, a lake, and then continue onto the next lake, called Lunken. From Lunken, continue onto Skjellbreidhytta, which is at 920 meters above sea level.

It's a bit of a climb up to Skjellbreidhytta at the end of the day in comparison to the start of the days, but there aren't any serious climbs on this route.

My notes

Today is a little bit of a slow start to the hike - it's great to get used to having a backpack on, since the trails are easy and pretty flat. Views are mostly forests with some open sections in between - if you squint during the second half of the day, you can see the mountains in the distance.

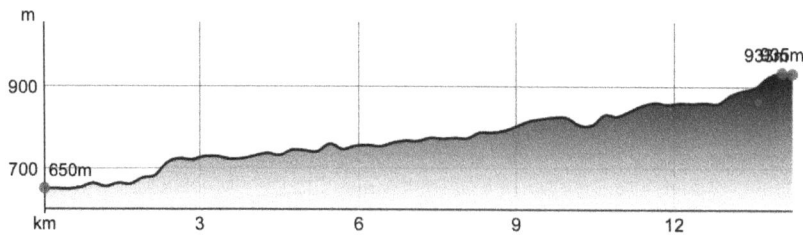

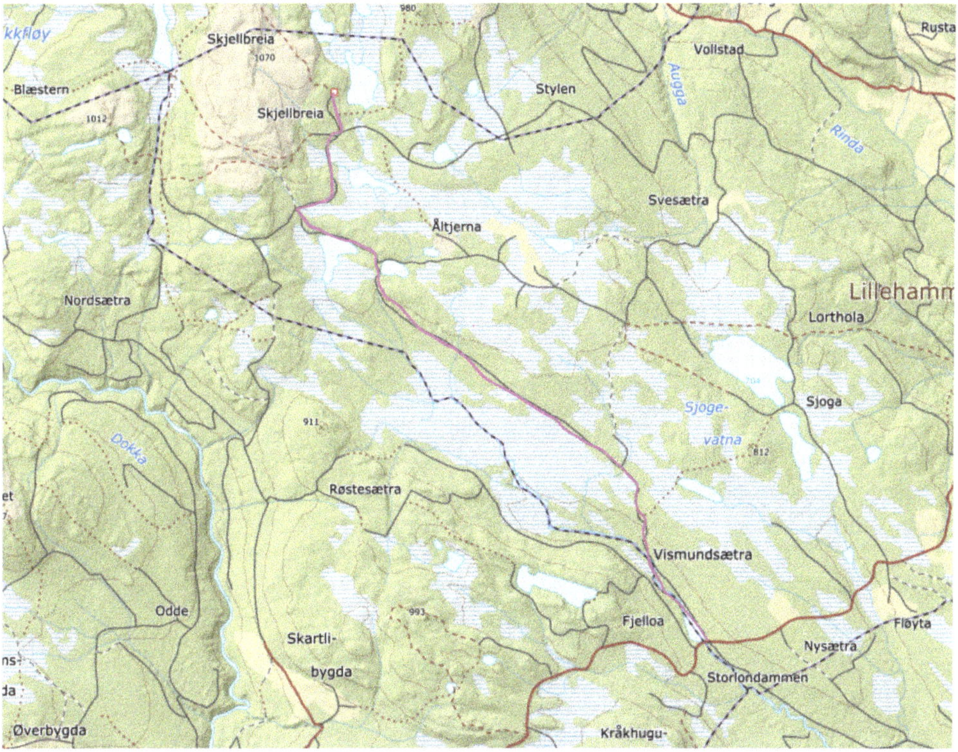

Skjellbreidhytta has a front porch that looks out onto the mountains around you - it's a great place to stop for lunch if you're combining the first two days

9

Skjellbreidhytta to Kittilbua

| 11.7 km | 316 meters | 415 meters | 4 hours |
| 7.3 miles | 1,036 feet | 1,361 feet | Moderate |

Today is the first day of the trip that's officially on the Jotunheimstien, which runs from Oslo's city center all the way to Jotunheimen. The trail first climbs through a forest, then goes into an open section. If you're lucky, you'll start to see the mountains in the distance here.

The trail continues to Nysetra, a small area with a few cabins. After this, the route turns towards the west, first along the lake Morgobeittjønnet and then in forest terrain until you reach Bentsetra. There's a short section along a road, and then the path turns off to the northwest to Kittilbua. It can be a little bit tough to see, so keep an eye out for the sign from the road.

My notes

It can be wet through this section, especially if it's rained recently - there's a bunch of myr, a Norwegian swamp land, and wetland in this section, and unlike the day before, you're not on the road to avoid it. There have been planks laid out to help avoid the wettest sections, but they sometimes get swallowed up by the swamp year over year.

The last bit is often the wettest - make sure you've got waterproof shoes on, and I recommend poles so that you can poke the ground and make sure it's not too wet.

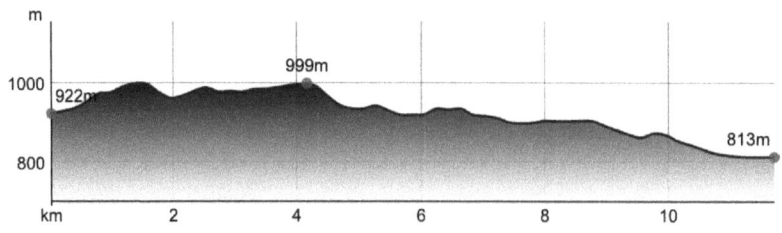

10

You'll be able to spot some mountains in the distance, but the first couple days are in flatter terrain

Kittilbua to Vestfjellhytta

| 17.2 km | 571 meters | 436 meters | 6.5 hours |
| 10.7 miles | 1,872 feet | 1,430 feet | Challenging |

Today is going to be a slow but gentle climb up to Vestfjellhytta from Kittilbua. Start by crossing over a small bridge west of the cabin, following a tractor road. Follow signs for Volden seter, a farm area, and then cross over another small bridge. From here, the terrain changes into more forested terrain.

Cross over the road and find the trail on the other side - it can be a bit difficult to spot. Follow Gamle Liomseterveg for 1.7 kilometers until it reaches a turnaround spot for buses. Follow signs further to Vestfjellhytta. From here, the trail passes through a bunch of sections that can be wet and marshy, so make sure you've got waterproof shoes. There can be running water on the trail if it's a wet season. Continue to follow the trail to Vestfjellhytta.

My notes

Vestfjellhytta has pretty spotty phone service - I was able to use my phone, but the others in the cabin couldn't. I recommend checking the weather and messages before you get to the cabin.

Today's route is still part of the Jotunheimstien, so you might share the cabin with people who are going on a very long hike. The cabin has good views out onto open areas near the cabin, and it feels a bit more on the wilderness than Kittilbua does.

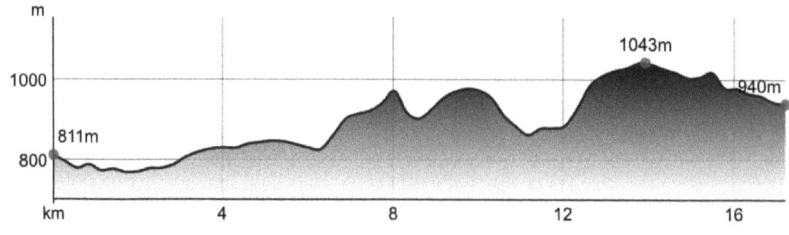

You might run into some trail friends on this section. Dogs need to be leashed in areas with sheep grazing

Vestfjellhytta to Liomseter

12.8 km	470 meters	442 meters	4 hours
8.0 miles	1,541 feet	1,449 feet	Moderate

Today's route continues on the Jotunheimstein, the route going from Oslo up to Jotunheimen national park. And like the days before, it continues to be a gentle path, but it can be quite marshy and wet.

The route starts going west through a series of farms, in open areas with views into the distance. There are routes and wooden walkways laid out to make it easier to navigate through the myr here. The path goes through a birch forest, then to a bridge over Revåa. If you're lucky, this area will be covered in wildflowers.

From here, it's easy to spot the path over Nordre Suluhøgda, 1122 meters - the first peak of the hike.

At about nine kilometers in, the trail meets another trail. Turn to the right and follow the signs towards Liomseter/Fehytta. Liomseter has no phone service, so you might want to pause at the top of Nordre Suluhøgda if you need to send any important messages.

My notes

The first serviced cabin on the way! Liomseter is a relatively quiet serviced cabin, but it attracts lots of families with children because Langsua is the easiest terrain to start doing cabin to cabin trips in. Enjoy your three-course dinner and a shower.

If you're outside of the main hiking or skiing season, you'll have to stay at Fehytta, which is a self-service cabin about 100 meters from Liomseter. There is a small cluster of cabins, so it can be a little bit difficult to find which one. Fehytta is a small cabin that was used for farming in the area, and it's more simple than some of the other self-service cabins.

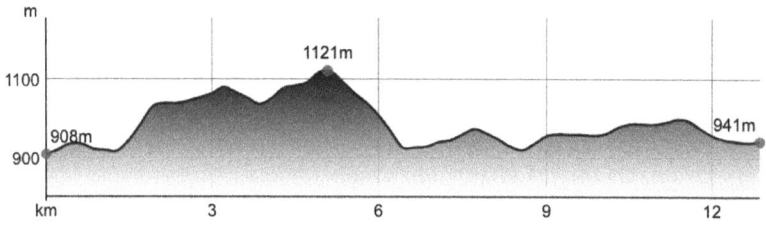

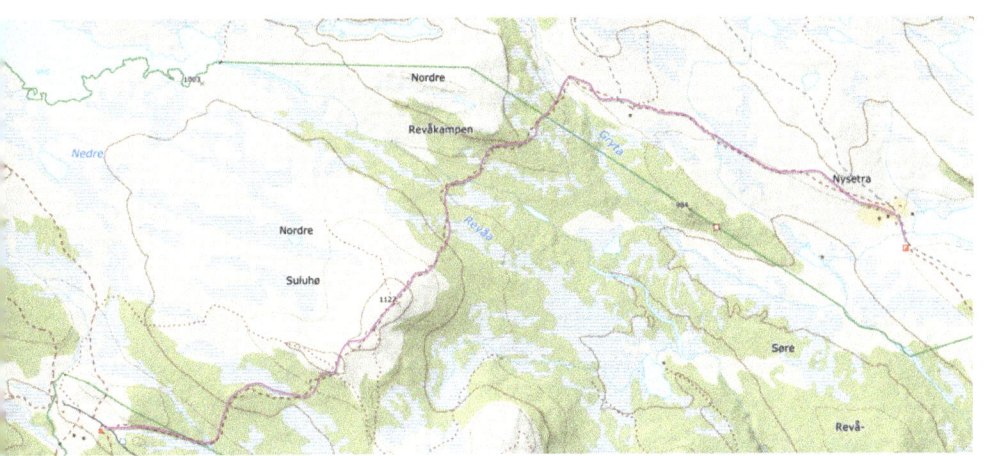

This section is great to do on skis in the winter. The elevation change is gradual, and the paths are some of the first ones marked in Norway

Liomseter to Storkvolvbua

| 14.5 km | 552 meters | 276 meters | 5 hours |
| 9.0 miles | 1,810 feet | 905 feet | Moderate |

Start today's hike by going towards Fehytta, then finding the right trail - there are three trails that branch off from the area. You want the middle trail towards Storkvolvbua (not the trail south towards Svarthamar or northeast towards Revsjøen).

The trail will start to gently climb through open mountain areas. There are lots of small ups and downs during the day, but no major climbs. If you're early in the year, you might want to wear long pants to avoid getting whipped by bushes as you go - it's generally easy to spot the trail, but there are a few places where it can be overgrown.

Eventually, the trail passes into high mountain terrain. The path has a few rocks on it, but it's generally pretty easy to walk.

My notes

I love Storkvolvbua - if you have a clear view, you have a view back towards all the areas you've already hiked, and the cabin feels like it's nestled into the mountains right next to a stream. This and the next day are when I felt like I was starting to really enter the mountains rather than the idyllic farmlands of the days before.

Same warnings as the days before - while the trail is generally dry and easy to walk on, there are some times that it can be wet or marshy.

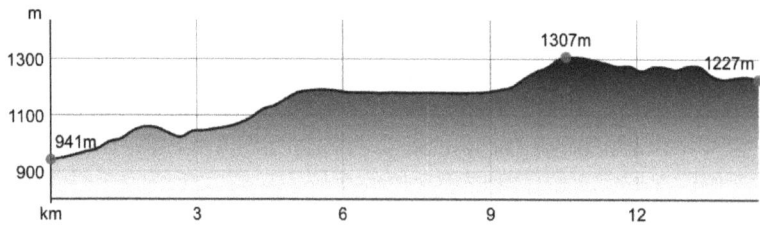

16

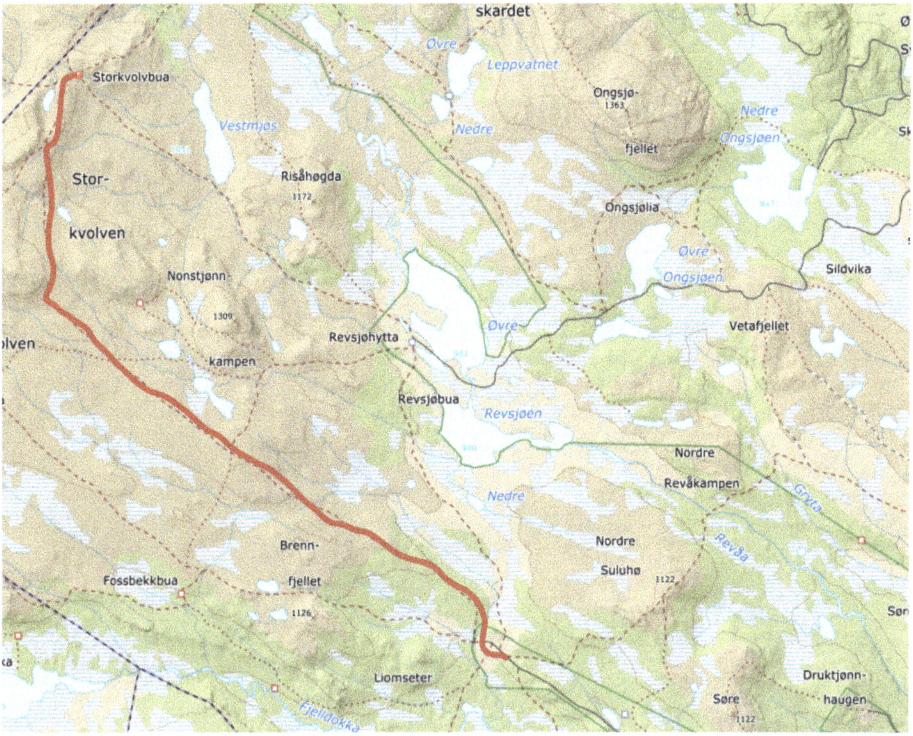

This section is very popular with families, and the cabin is equipped with plenty of board games.

Storkvolvbua to Storhøliseter

| 12.7 km | 304 meters | 531 meters | 4 hours |
| 7.9 miles | 997 feet | 1,741 feet | Moderate |

Start by going north towards Krusgravbekken, dropping elevation and looking back towards the Espedalsvatnet (Espedal lake) in the distance. The trail will turn towards the north, with a tiny climb after that. From there, the trail goes more or less straight northwest towards Størholiseter through easy to walk through terrain.

The trail is generally easy to find and follow, but again, there are a few spots that might be overgrown or wet depending on the year. There are plenty of spots to fill up on water along the way as well.

There is a cabin development that's about 200 meters before the actual cabin. Check UT or your map and keep going down the road until you actually reach Storhøliseter. It's in a fenced in collection of cabins, some of which are private and some of which are DNT.

My notes

This was where I started to feel like I was in the mountains again. I enjoyed this segment much more than I thought I would. Langsua is underrated if you can catch it in a dry summer.

It's pretty easy to combine the first few days of Omveien and do multiple segments in the same day, since the terrain is friendly and there's not much elevation gain. I would recommend combining days in this part rather than in the later parts of the trip - the terrain here is much easier than what's to come.

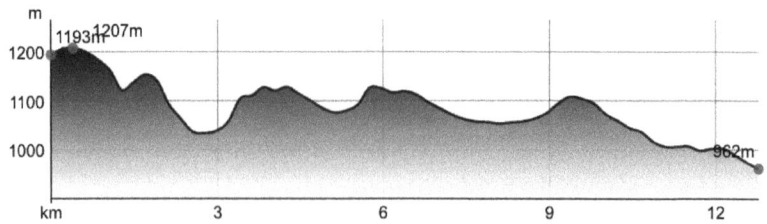

18

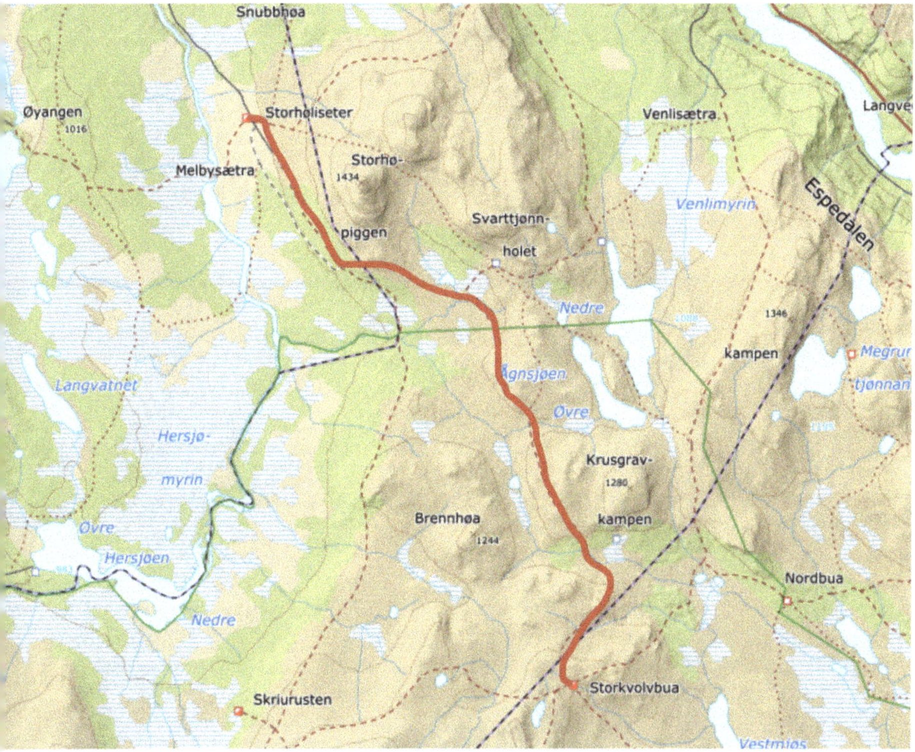

You can see the trail on the bottom right of the photo - it's dirt and easy to walk on. It's especially beautiful in the spring and fall, when you get either spring flowers or the fall colors

Storhøliseter to Oskampen

| 13.2km | 366 meters | 161 meters | 4 hours |
| 8.2 miles | 1,220 feet | 528 feet | Moderate |

Still on the Jotunheimstein! From Størholiseter, the trail drops down to Vinstra, then over a river via a summer bridge. This section can be a bit wet, but there are planks laid down at the worst spots.

After crossing the bridge, the route goes towards the west, with parts of the way on an old road. The trail is easy to follow and to walk on, but I ended up checking my phone a few times to make sure I was still supposed to be on the road.

Eventually, you go through a dam chute and then up to a road. Cross the road and look for the trail on the other side - it can be a bit difficult to spot, and you have to go about 100 meters on the road. From here, it's about an hour up to the cabin and a steady climb. As you climb up, the views get better and better. Eventually, Oskampen will appear in the distance, perched on the side of a lake and overlooking Jotunheimen.

My notes

You don't need to carry much water on this hike, since the trail passes numerous spots to get water. I also found it much less wet than the days before, partially because so much of the hike was on an old road. If you make it through the first part of the day with dry shoes, you're probably good to go.

I loved Oskampen and am sad I didn't spend the night here. The cabin is on the side of a lake with views out towards Jotunheimen. It's a small cabin, only 12 beds, but very comfortable, and that view.

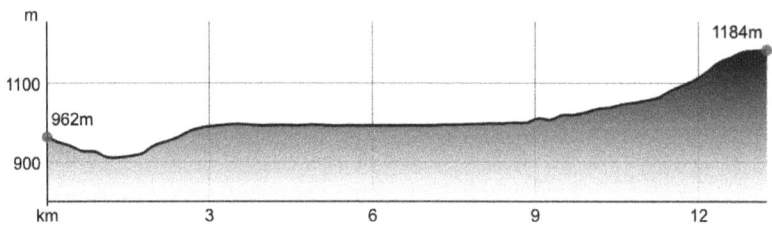

The paths through this section continue to be easy to hike on, and the elevation gain is quite manageable. If you want to combine days on the route, I suggest doing that in the first half of the route - the second half of the route is much longer and more technically challenging

Oskampen to Sikkilsdalsseter

| 11.1 km | 547 meters | 730 meters | 5 hours |
| 6.9 miles | 1,794 feet | 2,394 feet | Moderate |

The trail goes along the base of Oskampen the mountain, gently dropping elevation. The trail is dirt and pretty easy to follow here. It drops down to about 1,040 meters before crossing over a bridge over the river leading into Nedre Heimdalsvatnet.

From here, it's a climb up to the highest point on the Jotunheimstien, just below Vangstulkampen. The trail is easy to follow and not too rocky through this section. After passing the highest point, the trail drops down through open areas and then forests for 3.5 kilometers. After that, the trail pops out near Sikkilsdalsseter - although for the last 2km of the hike, the cabin appears closer than it actually is.

Some of the rivers on this section can be low if there isn't snow melt, so you may want to carry some water with you. If you're lucky enough to have dry weather, the views are fantastic.

My notes

This is a beautiful hike, and while there's quite a bit of elevation change, it's not technically difficult. Be careful on the last section - there are a couple of steep patches next to the river as you drop down, and there are also a couple of wet patches where it may be hard to see the next blaze on the trees.

Sikkilsdalsseter is a private cabin that works closely with DNT. You can book a room when you show up. It's a historic farm with several buildings and plenty of sleeping spots - the prices and structure are similar to a serviced DNT cabin.

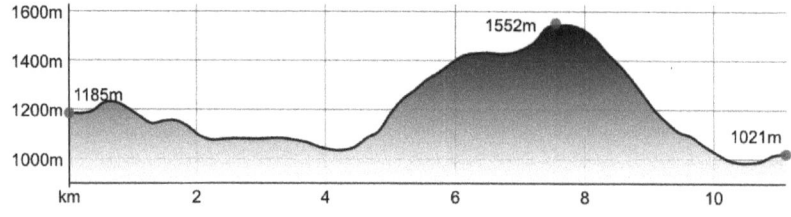

Sikkilsdalsseter to Gjendesheim

16.3 km
10.1 miles

906 meters
2,971 feet

904 meters
2,965 feet

8 hours
Challenging

Over Sikkilsdalsvatnet:

Start the day by going along the Sikkildals lake. Parts of the trail have large rocks that may require a bit of scrambling over. At the end of the lake, the trail will begin to climb up towards the Sikkilsdalsskardet, with a view towards Jotunheimen.

After the small climb, start to follow a path through a combination of open area and forest towards Maurvangen. The path is easy to follow, but there can be a few streams to rock hop across if there's been rain recently.

Eventually, the route drops down to Maurvangen. Walk through the camping area towards the reception area, then cross over the pedestrian bridge to the road. Cross the road and turn right, then turn left onto the road towards Gjendesheim.

From here, it's about half an hour on a road to Gjendesheim. There is a trail beside the road to Gjendesheim that's not marked on the map - look on the right for a turnoff to catch it

Over Sikkilsdalshø (map and elevation profile)

I chose to go over Sikkilsdalshø, which takes about 8 hours and has quite a bit more climb. To do that trail, start by climbing up from behind Sikkilsdalsseter. The trail goes through a combination of forest and open mountain areas, then reaches a lake and goes along the lake for a bit.

After the lake, there's a final rocky climb - the path isn't super wide, so watch your footing. At the top, there's a spectacular view out towards Jotunheimen. After that, the trail drops elevation through first rocky and then dirt terrain. It's a bit steep but not terrible, and the views are fantastic. Eventually, the path starts to go through the forest and then meets up with the trail coming via Sikkilsdalsvatnet.

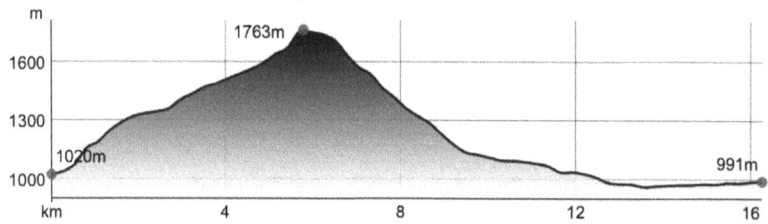

My notes:

I absolutely loved the route over Sikkildalshø - the views were spectacular. I highly recommend it if you've got good weather. There are a few false summits on the way and a little bit of scrambling, but it's not bad. (And Gjendesheim has two dinner seatings, so there's no rush to get there.)

It's longer than I mentally expected from where the two trails meet up to Gjendesheim. Try to find the trail alongside the road on the way to Gjendesheim if you can - it's much more pleasant than the road. Alternatively, you might be able to catch the shuttle bus from the boat parking area to the cabin.

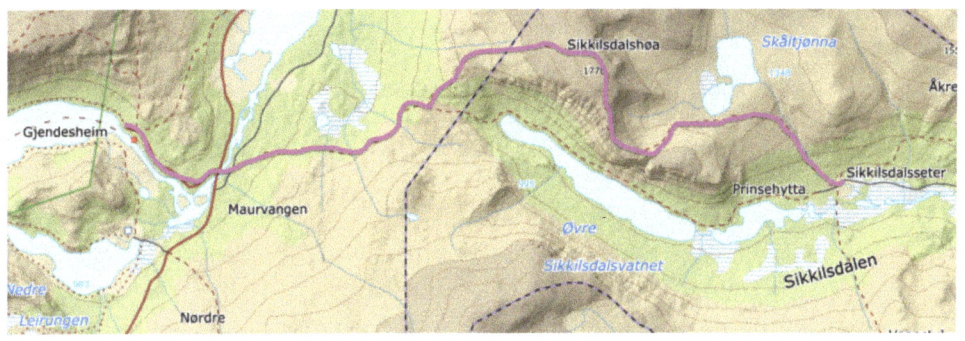

Gjendesheim to Glitterheim

| 21.8 km | 969 meters | 582 meters | 8 hours |
| 13.5 miles | 3,178 feet | 1,909 feet | Challenging |

The route for today starts by going up towards Gjendehalsen, passing by the paths that branch off to Besseggen and Memurubu. There's a climb at the beginning of the day as you pass by the trail that branches off towards Besseggen. It can be a bit rocky in this section.

Keep going towards the north, passing by the ends of a few lakes. You should have a great view out towards Glittertinden through this section.

Pass over the bridge at the end of the Russvatnet, then turn towards the west, gently climbing along the riverside and then up onto a bowl. There is one bridge here that is a hanging bridge that really bounces as you cross it - it's stable, but it's a bit nervewracking to go over.

The terrain becomes more open and rocky here as the trail climbs away from the river. The trail continues to gain elevation up to a saddle in between eastern and western Hestlægerhøe ("Austre og Vestre Hestlægerhøe").

After that, drop down towards Glitterheim, first in rocky terrain and then in partially wet terrain. The cabin is further away than it appears from the mountain, and there's a little bit of a detour towards the end.

My hiking notes

This is a long hike with some sneaky elevation in it - there's not a climb like there is on some of the other days here, but I definitely felt it by the end of the day. I found the end the mentally toughest - you can see Glitterheim with a few kilometers left to go.

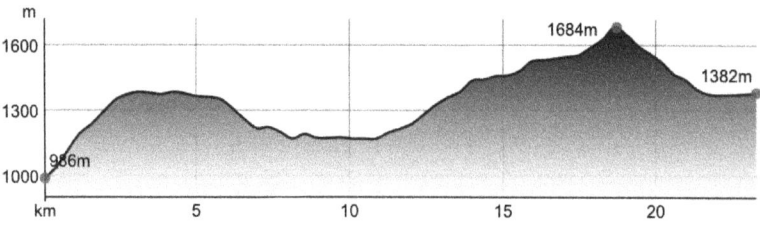

There were lots of lakes and rivers underway to fill up a water bottle in, plus views onto a lot more lakes

Glitterheim to Spiterstulen - Glittertinden

↗

↘

| 17.2 km
10.7 miles | 1,378 meters
4,520 feet | 1,672 meters
5,484 feet | 9 hours
Very Challenging |

Ready to take on Norway's second highest peak?

Start the day by taking the trail directly behind Glitterheim. It starts out on dirt trails, which quickly change into rockier trails. Continue climbing, taking your time to balance on the rocks as you go. As the trail gets closer to the top, it starts to cross across snow fields. Follow the marked trail and stay away from the side of the snowfield.

There is no marker for the summit, but I recommend sitting down anywhere on the snow and enjoying the view. There's a stunning view back towards the surrounding peaks.

The trail down to Spiterstulen is easy to find, but it's quite steep and rocky for the first few kilometers. I found it took as long as the hike towards the top. After dropping through the rocky section, the trail continues through a flat section for a couple of kilometers before turning slightly and starting the hike down along the wall towards Spiterstulen.

The trail hits the road. Turn left and follow it to Spiterstulen.

My notes

I loved this hike. The view is spectacular, and while it's quite a climb, it's not too technically challenging. I was glad to have my sitting pad for a long lunch break at the top.

This is a popular day tour from Glitterheim, so you may see quite a few other people out with much smaller backpacks. Make sure that you have enough layers, because it is cold at the top. And if you're not going all the way to Spiterstulen, borrow a sled from Glitterheim for the fastest possible way down the mountain.

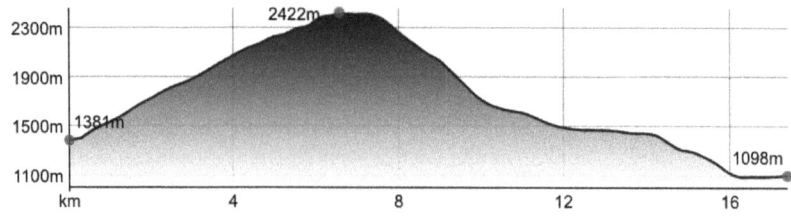

Don't walk too close to the edge while close to the top - there can be snow overhangs hiding steep drops

Glitterheim to Spiterstulen - not Glittertinden

15.9 km **9.8 miles**	↗ **365 meters** **1,197 feet**	↘ **663 meters** **2,175 feet**	**5 hours** **Challenging**

This is a slightly easier alternative to going over Glittertinden from Glitterheim to Spiterstulen. It's easier in that there's much less elevation gain, but it's in no way an easy trail - the terrain is rocky, and there are places where you'll need to rock hop across rivers.

Start by crossing over a summer bridge over the Steinbuelve, going into the Veodalen valley. The first 4.5 kilometers are a gentle climb through the valley. The trail crosses over a few rivers that may need to be rock hopped or waded across, particularly if there's been recent snow melt.

From here, the trail starts to curve more towards the north and steeply climb up towards right under the Veslglupen. The trail goes past a series of small lakes, heading west, then curves towards the northwest again.

At about 8.7 total kilometers, there's another river that requires wading. Cross that river, then continue to follow the trail, gently dropping elevation. Eventually, the trail meets up with the trail coming over Glittertinden. From here, follow the trail along the side of a valley and then down to Spiterstulen.

<u>My notes</u>

I recommend doing the trail over Glittertinden if you can - the views are absolutely spectacular. This isn't to shame this trail, which is also beautiful, but Glittertinden was one of my favorite hikes in Norway.

If there's been a lot of recent snow melt or rain, ask at the cabin about how much wading is required. It varies a lot depending on the time of year and recent weather.

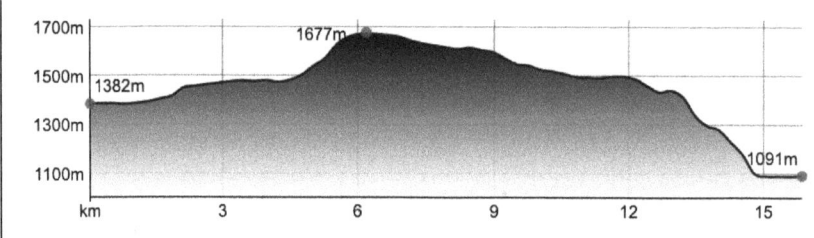

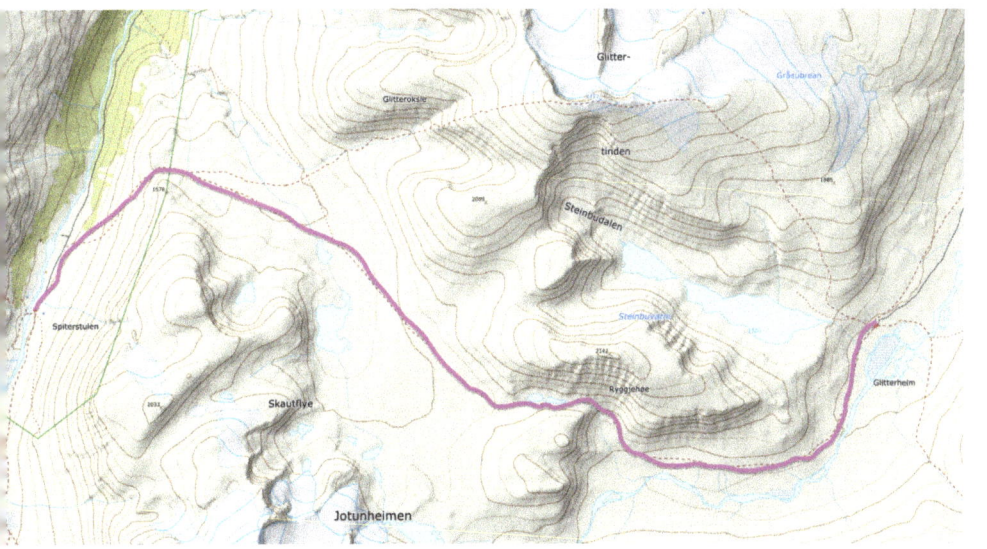

The last drop down to Spiterstulen can be mentally tough if you're not expecting it - be prepared for it to feel longer than it looks on the map

Spiterstulen to Leirvassbu

| 15.9 km | 458 meters | 147 meters | 5 hours |
| 9.9 miles | 1,502 feet | 482 feet | Challenging |

The route starts going south from Spiterstulen, following the river. The trail starts as a dirt trail that's pretty easy to follow, but there are a few sections where it's rocky. Keep going south, gradually adding elevation.

At about six kilometers in, there's a fork in the trail. Turn towards the west and follow the trail going to Leirvassbu - there's a sign. From here, the trail can get rocky. As you get close to Leirvassbu, you'll circle around a lake, Leirvatnet, towards the cabin. This area can have quite a few bugs if it's still.

If it's rained recently, there may be some areas where you have to wade or jump across rocks. I found those mostly in the second half of the hike - there were planks put out for the sections in the first part of the hike.

My notes

This is a good day to make into a bit of a rest day in the middle of the hike, especially if you've added in Galdhøpiggen the day before. You're up at considerably higher elevation for a lot of the day - when I hiked it, the lakes were still mostly frozen, and the snowmelt made the rivers very high.

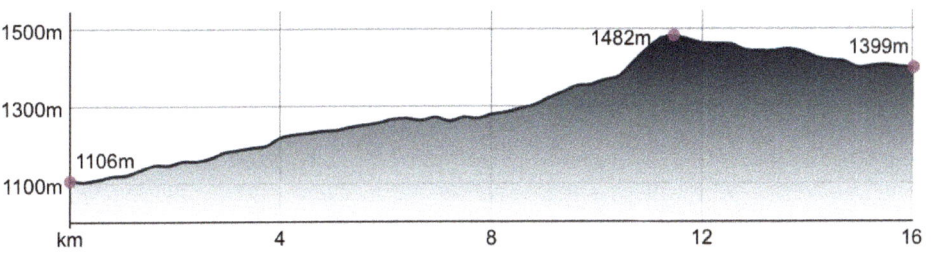

This trail can have snowfields until very late in the season - I found poles to be helpful on the snowy sections, though not in the places where the snow had melted to reveal the rocks underneath

Leirvassbu to Olavsbu

| 10.6 km | 363 meters | 327 meters | 3.5 hours |
| 6.6 miles | 1,191 feet | 1,073 feet | Challenging |

My hiking notes

The day starts by going along a construction road from Leirvassbu towards Sognefjellshytta and Skogadalsbøen. The path is a bit tricky to find in this section, especially if there are still snowfields on the ground. I ended up getting a little off path and catching the path again about a kilometer in. Keep checking UT.

At about two kilometers in, the trail passes by the turnoff to Kyrkja. From here, it passes by two lakes, upper and lower Høgvagltjønnen, before reaching a fork. Take the trail on the right towards Olavsbu, not the one on the left towards Gjendebu. From here, it's six kilometers in rocky terrain. There's a bit of a climb, then a gradual downhill until you reach Olavsbu. Olavsbu feels like it comes out of nowhere, so don't get discouraged if you don't see the cabin until a few hundred meters away.

There were still a lot of snowfields left when I did this hike, and there were a few sections where I had to rock hop across running water. My poles were definitely helpful.

My notes

You can combine this hike with the hike to Skogadalsbøen if you get an early start or are feeling really good - the next day is all downhill.

Olavsbu is an enormous self-service cabin - it's DNT Oslo's biggest self-service cabin. There's usually a hyttevakt, or a volunteer who helps make sure the cabin runs smoothly, there if you have questions.

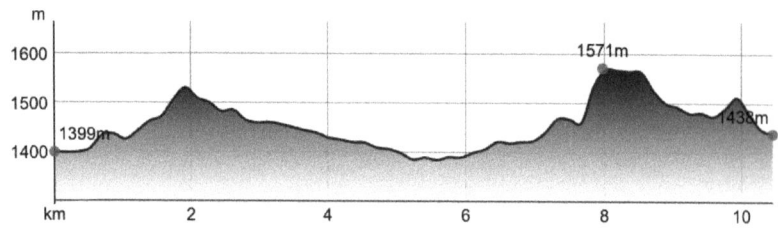

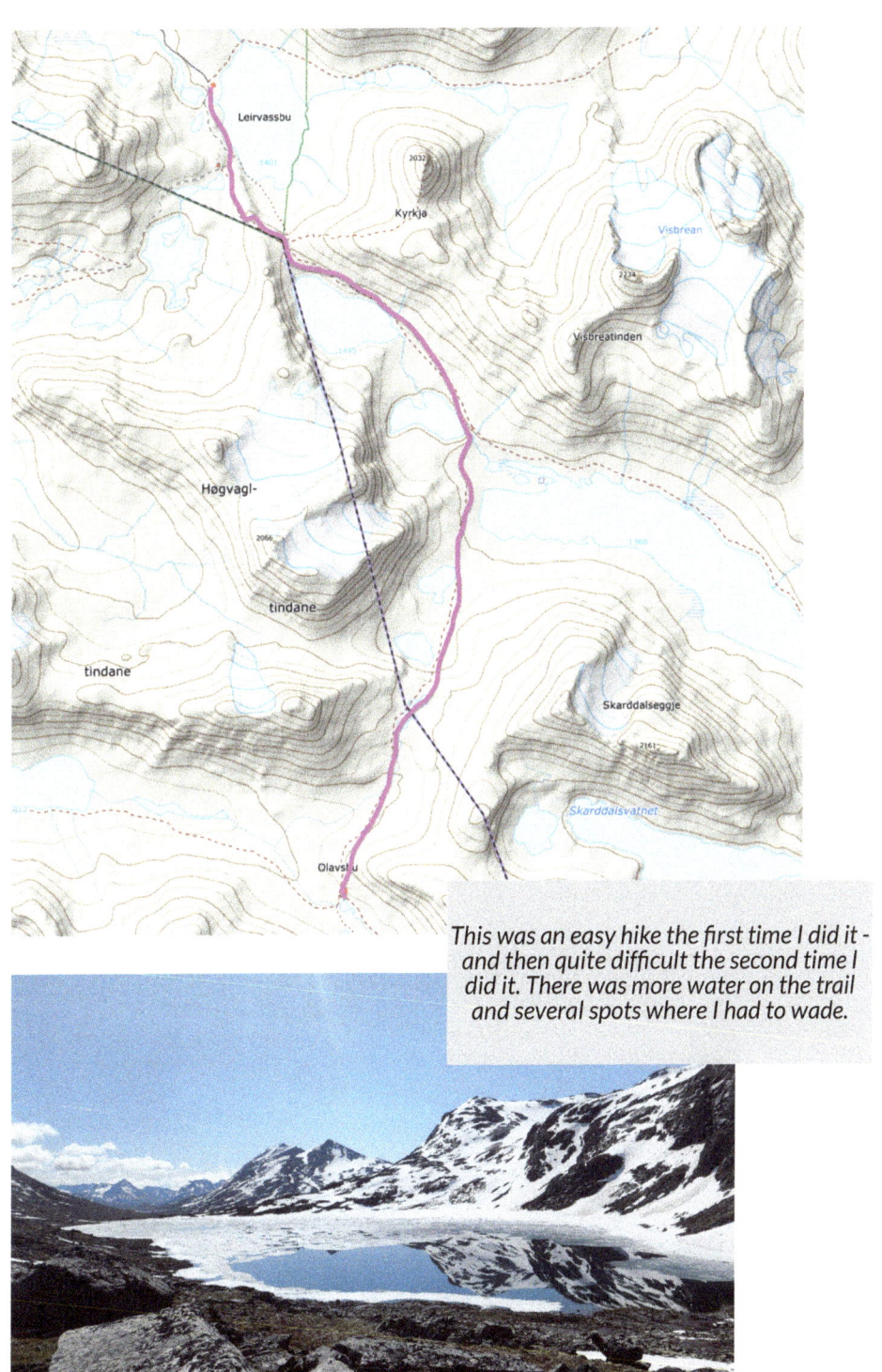

This was an easy hike the first time I did it -
and then quite difficult the second time I
did it. There was more water on the trail
and several spots where I had to wade.

Olavsbu to Skogadalsbøen - Skogadalen

 ↗ ↘

| 17.2 km | 330 meters | 930 meters | 6 hours |
| 10.7 miles | 1,082 feet | 3,050 feet | Challenging |

There are two paths from Olavsbu to Skogadalsbøen - you can also take the route over Rauddalen and Storutladalen.

The trail starts by going northwest from Olavsbu through some rockier terrain near the cabin. Continue for about three kilometers until you reach the south side of the Rauddalsvatnet. About halfway along the Rauddalsvatnet, there's an intersection. The trail over Skogadalen turns off to the left / south, turning sharply south.

The trail climbs up and over a ridge. The elevation gain feels more intense than it looks on the map. Drop down on the south side of the ridge. The trail intersects with the trail from Gjendebu to Skogadalsbøen. Turn towards the west, going along the south side of a series of small lakes. This section can be rocky. From here, the trail continues to drop elevation, eventually entering the Skogadal valley.

There are about five kilometers in the forest before you reach the cabin - it can feel mentally longer than it looks on the map, especially at the end of a day of hiking. The trail drops directly into the cabin complex at the end of the day. You'll pass by a great place to jump into the river and go swimming next to a large bridge, about 100 meters before the cabin.

My notes

I preferred the route through the Rauddalen because it was in open mountain terrain for longer, so I felt like I had more views out onto the surrounding mountains. Both are great hikes, though.

There may be some rivers that you need to rock hop across here, especially if it's rained recently or there's a lot of snow melt.

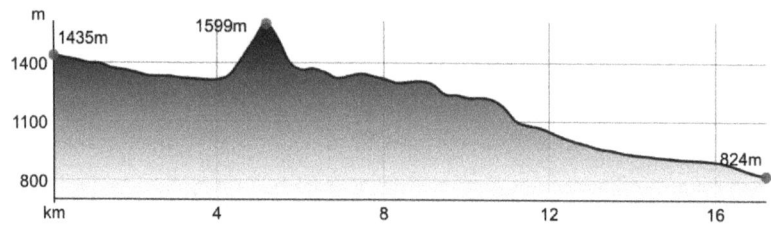

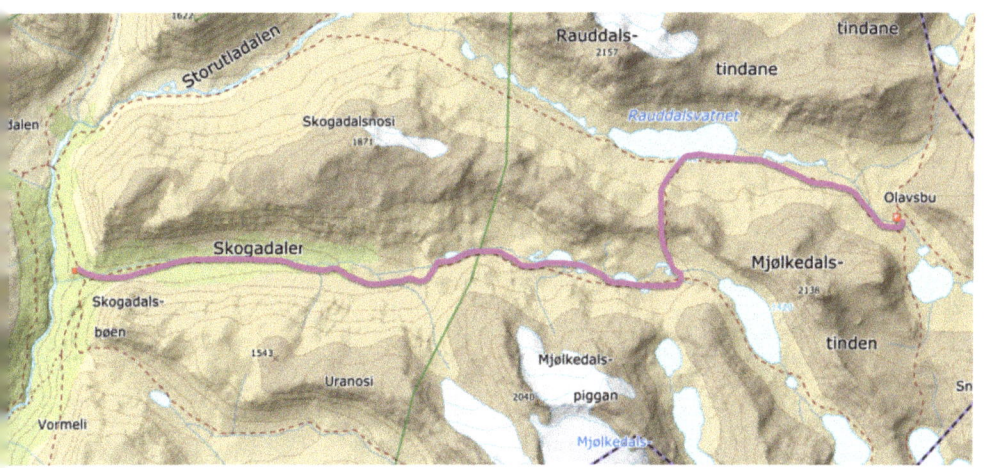

The valleys around Skogadalsbøen are generally full of plant and animal life - I hiked the whole day here listening to birds chirping and smelling wildflowers

Olavsbu to Skogadalsbøen-Rauddalen/Storutladalen

| 18.2 km | 232 meters | 839 meters | 6 hours |
| 11.3 miles | 2,761 feet | 2,752 feet | Challenging |

This route is a gentle downhill for most of the day - and it's even in friendly terrain, so it's a good change from the more intense hikes the days before.

The trail starts by going northwest from Olavsbu through some rockier terrain near the cabin. Continue for about three kilometers until you reach the south side of the Rauddalsvatnet. From here, continue to follow the trail along the lake, continuing as the lake turns into a river. It's pretty flat through the section, although the terrain is a bit rocky.

From here, the trail starts to curve towards the west as you enter Storutladalen, a valley leading to Skogadalsbøen. The trail continues to drop elevation, with some flatter sections mixed with some steeper ones. The terrain changes into a dirt trail with plants and some small trees around you. Continue to follow the south side of the river until the trail turns towards the south.

From here, it's about 2.5 kilometers to Skogadalsbøen in a flat section through the valley.

My hiking notes

This is a really lovely hike if you've got nice weather. There were wildflowers along the trail, birds chirping, and a birch forest towards the end. The views were spectacular the whole way. There's no sections that are technically challenging, just long.

I prefer this route to the route over Skogadalen. The other route is in the forest for longer, so I didn't feel that I had the same fantastic views.

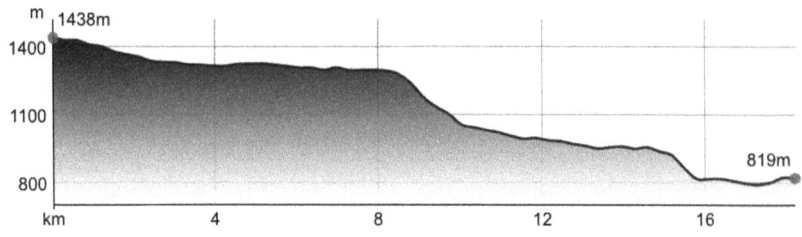

The cabin appears seemingly out of nowhere as you get closer. I kept wondering where it was and whether I really only had a few hundred meters to go, and then it just showed up.

Skogadalsbøen to Vettismorki

10.2 km
6.3 miles

551 meters
1,807 feet

700 meters
2,296 feet

5 hours
Challenging

Start the trail going south from Skogadalsbøen, following signs towards Vettis or Vettismorki. The trail is mostly flat until you cross over a bridge over the Uradøla. From here, the trail starts to climb, first in dirt and then in rocky terrain. It's four kilometers of climbing, so pace yourself. The views out into the valley are spectacular through this section, especially as you get into the rockier terrain.

At the midpoint of the trail, about 5.2 kilometers in, the trail starts to drop elevation. The way down is steeper than the way up - there's a fairly steep descent for another 2.5 kilometers before the trail flattens out slightly. The terrain is a mixture of rocky and dirt through here.

Eventually, the trail flattens out and starts to go towards Vettismorki. It can be wet through this section - watch where you're stepping. Vettismorki is in the middle of a patch of private cabins, so check the door signs to make sure you've got the right one.

My notes

There's actually quite a bit of climb involved in this hike - more than I initially expected from the map and trail description. The high point of the trail is at almost the perfect middle of the trail. The views were much better than I expected - you're up high enough to have an overview of all of the surrounding mountains.

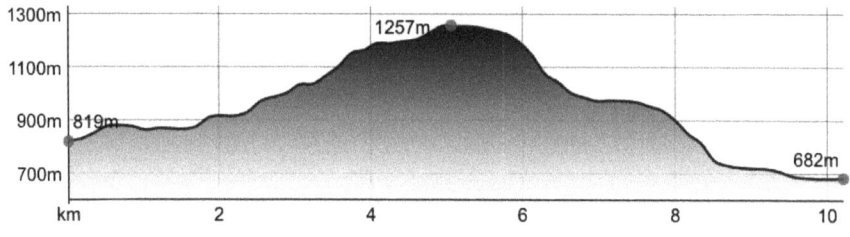

It is possible to do this as a day hike from Skogadalsbøen, going out and back to Vettismorki, but it's a very long day.

41

Vettismorki to Hjelle

2.7 km 1.7 miles	77 meters 252 feet	464 meters 1,521 feet	4 hours Moderate

From Vettismorki, follow signs to Vettisfossen, one of Norway's most famous waterfalls. It's only 1.2 kilometers to the waterfall on friendly trails, so you can even incorporate it with the day before if you're feeling good.

Stop and admire the waterfall. After that, the trail drops steeply through the forest until you reach Vetti Gard, a historic farming complex. Once you pass Vetti Gard, the trail continues to drop steeply for another hundred meters of elevation before flattening out a bit. From here, start going along a farm road towards Hjelle, which is a large parking lot for people going for hikes in the area.

During the summers, there's a morning bus that takes hikers from Hjelle to Øvre Årdal or Turtagrø. If there's no bus, just keep following the road until you reach Øvre Årdal (or until you can convince a cabin friend to give you a ride).

My hiking notes

Vettisfossen is really impressive - there's a viewing platform so that you can appreciate how big it actually is. If you're not going all the way to Øvre Årdal, it's worth making the detour from Vettismorki.

The end of the day here is a little bit boring along the road. If there are other hikers, you might be able to catch a ride with them.

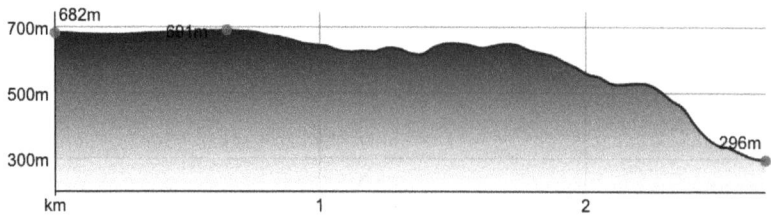

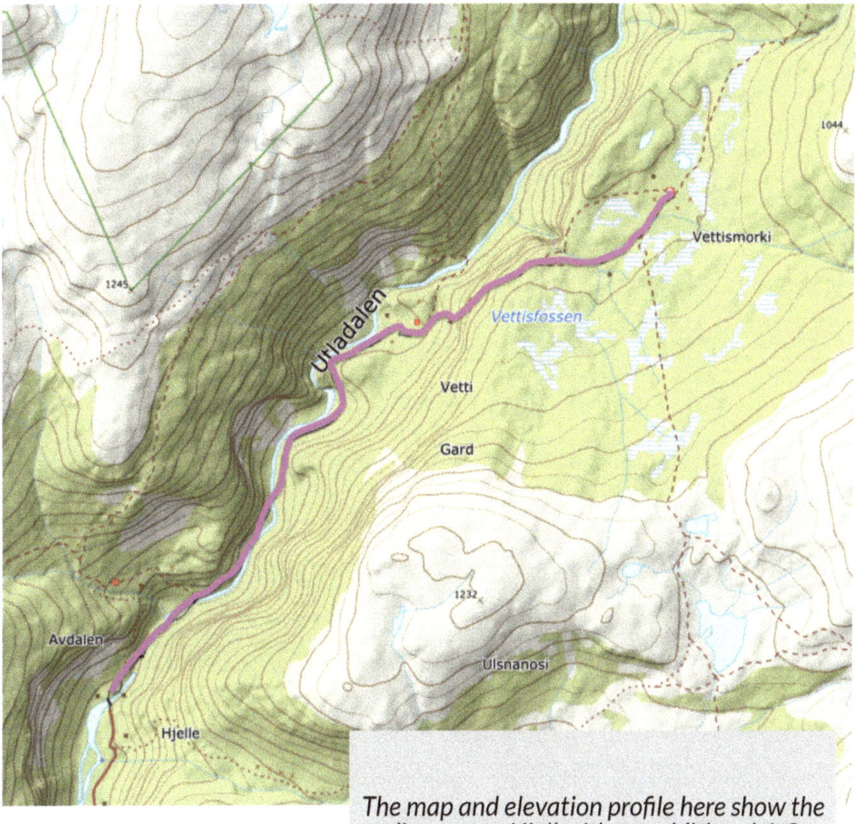

The map and elevation profile here show the distance to Hjelle. It's an additional 6-8 kilometers on the road back to Øvre Årdal

43

Extensions

If you're looking to add some more detours into your Omveien trip, you can add in some of Norway's highest or most iconic summits:

- Besseggen is Norway's most visited hike - more than 50,000 people a year hike it. It features an iconic view of two lakes on a mountain ridge and is easy to add in from Gjendesheim.

- Galdhøpiggen is Norway's highest peak at 2,469 meters. It's a long and steep hike, but it's not too technically challenging - you'll see families out doing it, and you can sled down if you've got some snowfields left.

- Kyrkja is a distinctive, church spire shaped mountain outside Leirvassbu. It's a short distance of a hike, but it's extremely steep and requires mountain experience and sure footing.

Hike	Distance (km)	Up (meters)	Down (meters)	Time	Level
Besseggen	13.3	1,076	1,086	6-8 hours	Very challengin
Galdhøpiggen	13.8	1,754	1,754	8 hours	Challenging
Kyrkja	8.8	603	603	4 hours	Very challengin

Fjellvettreglene (Norwegian Mountain Code)

The Norwegian Mountain Code contains the guidelines for having a safe trip in the Norwegian mountains. They're considered an important part of Norwegian cultural heritage and were introduced after a spate of fatal accidents in 1950.

1. Plan your trip and inform others about the route you have selected.

2. Adapt the planned routes according to ability and conditions.

3. Pay attention to the weather and the avalanche warnings.

4. Be prepared for bad weather and frost, even on short trips.

5. Bring the necessary equipment so you can help yourself and others.

6. Choose safe routes. Recognize avalanche terrain and unsafe ice.

7. Use a map and a compass. Always know where you are.

8. Don't be ashamed to turn around.

9. Conserve your energy and seek shelter if necessary.

Besseggen

| 13.3 km | 1,076 meters | 1,086 meters | 6-8 hours |
| 8.3 miles | 3,529 feet | 3,526 feet | Very challenging |

This is Norway's most done hike and one of National Geographic's ten hikes to do in your life, and you should definitely add it to your list.

I recommend starting the hike from Memurubu so that you don't have to worry about catching a boat back to Gjendesheim at the end of the day. Either spend the night at Memurubu or take the first boat from Gjendesheim in the morning to start the hike. From Memurubu, the hike starts with a very steep climb on a dirt trail for about two kilometers. Here, you pass by a trail going towards Glitterheim. Continue towards the east, in what quickly becomes more rocky and rolling terrain.

You'll pass signs in this section that let you know how you're pacing, and whether you should turn around based on your speed.

Continue climbing. The trail passes by a small lake, with spectacular views over the Gjendevatnet to your right. Continue following the trail over a small descent until you reach the side of the Bessvatnet lake.

From here, the trail continues on a short but very steep section. This section requires climbing on hands and knees, and there are drop offs on each side. Put away hiking poles if you have them and make sure to keep your center of gravity low as you climb. It's a short section, a few hundred meters, that's particularly challenging.

If it is raining or you are not comfortable, you can instead choose to do a longer loop around Bessvatnet to meet the trail from Glitterheim. That trail is not easy - it still goes on rocky terrain - but does not have a steep drop off on either side.

From the top of the scramble, stop and look back to see the classic view with Gjendevatnet on one side and Bessvatnet on the other.

After this, continue along a flat section for about a kilometer. This section is a wide trail on top of the mountain and easy to walk. After that, start the drop down towards Gjendesheim. This is quite steep and goes over rocky terrain. Make sure to stay on the trail - there are several areas where people have tried to create shortcuts in the terrain. End at Gjendesheim.

I thought that this hike was going to be overhyped just given its sheer popularity. It was not. The views were absolutely spectacular, and it's well worth doing. That being said, I would only do it in good weather - the scramble is difficult if the rocks are wet, and it can be crowded with people who are not experienced in the mountains.

Make sure to have clothes that are suitable for both high elevation and lower down. You'll sweat a lot on the way up and want something warmer to change into for the flatter sections along the top of the ridge.

If you're a fast hiker and have good weather, think about starting in the afternoon rather than the morning - I had many fewer people on the route because I started around one rather than in the morning with the boat.

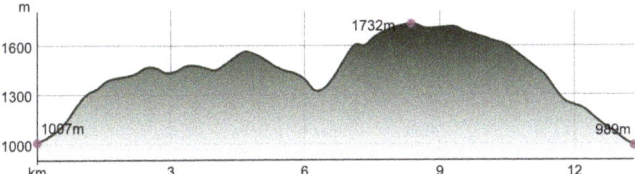

Spiterstulen to Galdhøpiggen

| 13.8 km | 1,754 meters | 1,754 meters | 8 hours |
| 8.6 miles | 5,753 feet | 5,753 feet | Challenging |

Galdhøpiggen is Norway's highest mountain and an important part of Norwegian culture - its elevation, 2469, is immediately recognizable to many people. (UT.no claims it's recognizable for all Norwegians, but that might be a stretch.)

It's a straightforward, though challenging, hike up from Spiterstulen to the summit. Take the trail from Spiterstulen, cross the river, and immediately start climbing. The beginning of the day is on dirt trails, which quickly turn into rocky terrain. Continue to climb and you will likely encounter snowfields. Fortunately, this is a well-traveled path, so there should be clear footprints marking the trail.

Continue to steadily climb until you reach the summit. There's a small cafe at the summit that offers sausages, coffee, and other warm drinks. Stop here and enjoy the view. When you're done, turn around and go down the way you came.

My notes

This is a very easy trail to follow, but it is quite a lot of climbing. It is no way an easy hike, but you'll see plenty of families with children on the way.

There are two false summits on the way - I kept thinking that I could see the peak and was almost there, only to realize that there was another peak hiding behind the first. Mentally prepare yourself for that.

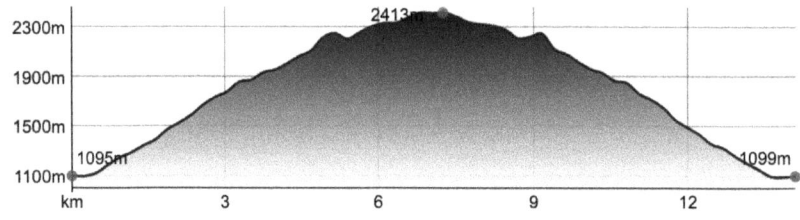

If you have snowfields, you can save some time on the descent by sliding down on your butt. It is not elegant, but it is a lot of fun.

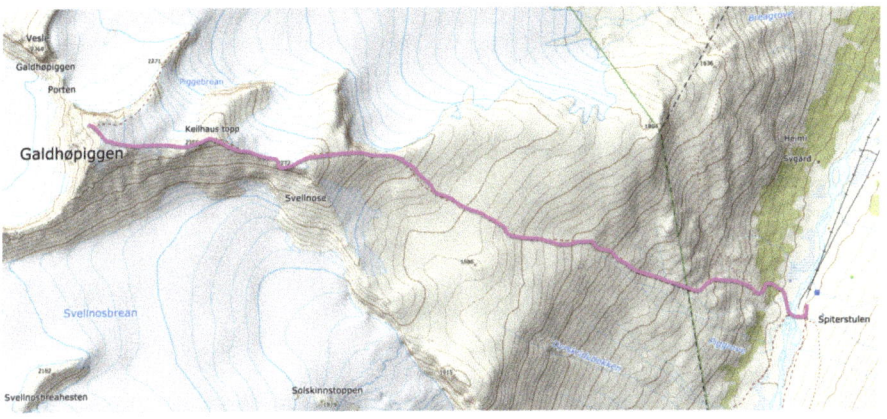

Leirvassbu to Kyrkja

8.8 km
5.5 miles

603 meters
1,978 feet

603 meters
1,978 feet

4 hours
Very challenging

Kyrkja is an iconic mountain top in Norway - it spikes up from the surrounding terrain. It's a spectacular trip, but it's only recommended for adults and those with mountain experience - it's very steep, and there's quite a bit of scrambling at the end.

The first two kilometers of the trail follows the road from Leirvassbu towards Olavsbu. The trail can be a bit hard to find here, and there are often still snowfields. After about two kilometers, there is a turnoff to the left for the trail up to Kyrkja. It's not marked with the red T, but there are clear cairns to show the trail.

The terrain in this section is extremely rocky and steep. As you get close to the top, you will need to scramble on all fours through some sections. The trail is narrow, with steep drop offs on both sides. I don't recommend this hike in the rain.

Once you reach the top, take a look around and then go back the way you came.

My notes

I left my backpack and poles next to a cairn when I still had about 400 meters of elevation to climb. That was a great idea - the last section is extremely steep, and I felt like I was clinging to the rocks on the side of the mountain. Not having the backpack made me more flexible and kept my center of gravity closer to the mountain.

The view from the top was well worth it, but this is definitely not a hike to do if you aren't comfortable with scrambling or are scared of heights.

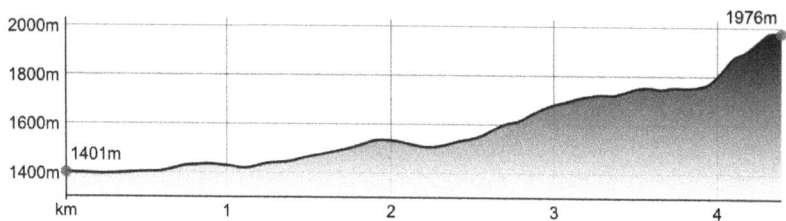

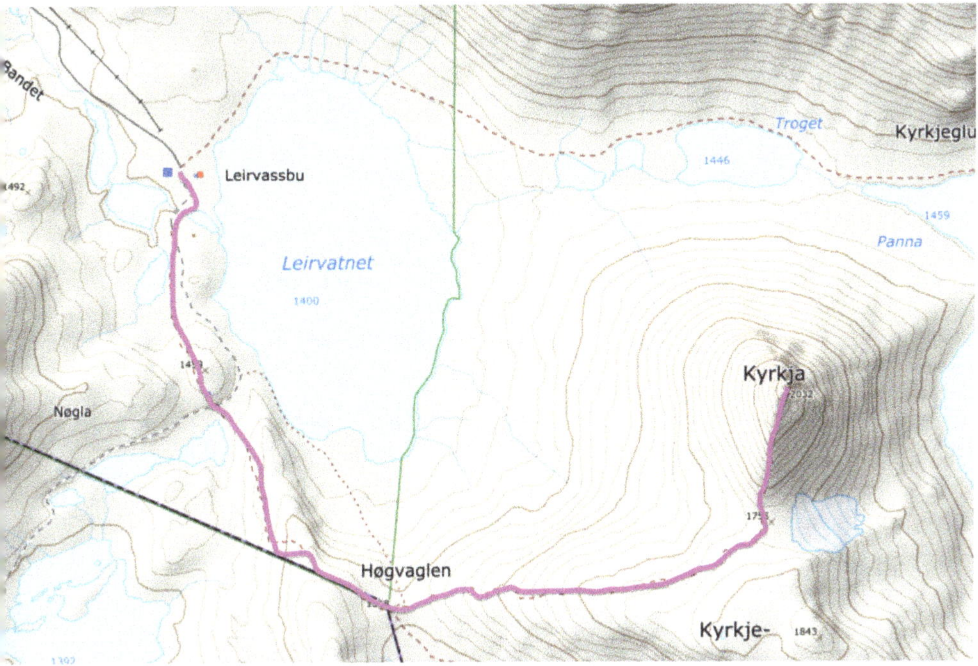

Randet

Troget

Kyrkjeglu

Leirvassbu

1446

1459

Panna

Leirvatnet

1400

Kyrkja

1492

2032

Nøgla

1472

1725

Høgvaglen

1372

Kyrkje-

1843

1392

I was treated to a fighter jet flyover when I finally reached the top of the scramble - quite a surprise after hiking in silence

Logistics

Getting There and Back

To get to Storlondommen for the start of the hike, you can take the public bus from Lillehammer train station. The enTUR app has the latest times and routes. Note that there are usually only three daily departures from Lillehammer to Storlondommen, and the service may not run every day. If you need to take a taxi, you can call one online through Lillehammer taxi, and it's about $60.

At the end of the hike, you'll end in Øvre Årdal. From here, you can take the bus to Tutragrø once a day during the peak season if you want to continue hiking through northern Jotunheimen or Breheimen. You can also take the bus to Lom or Sogndal to catch transport back to Oslo and Bergen.

If you are looking for drop points throughout the hike, here are the cabins that are possible to get to with public transportation:

- **Liomseter:** during the summers and peak winter season, there is a twice-weekly bus from Liomseter to Lillehammer or reverse. Check their website for the latest details. Outside of those times, you'll have to take a taxi to get there.

- **Gjendesheim:** Gjendesheim has regular bus service to Oslo and fairly frequent bus service to Lom when the road is open (e.g. not during parts of the winters). Tickets to Oslo need to be booked in advance, while tickets to Lom do not. This is one of the easiest places to exit or enter the hike from, and I recommend using Gjendesheim as your drop point if you want to split the hike into sections.

- **Spiterstulen:** line 201 goes from Spiterstulen to Lom twice daily during peak hiking season. Lom has a variety of bus connections to other destinations in Norway.

- **Leirvassbu:** bus line 203 goes twice daily during peak hiking season. It goes from Leirvassbu to Lom, where you can catch connections back to the rest of Norway.

Luggage Transport

There is no luggage transport along this hike. If you choose to add in Besseggen as an extension, you can leave your bag at Gjendesheim for the day.

Supplies

If you're planning to camp, bring the food that you need with you. There are places to buy supplies in all of the serviced cabins, but they are generally small kiosks that only sell snacks and a couple of varieties of freeze-dried food. Lillehammer has numerous grocery stores - search "matbutikk" in Google Maps. They don't always come up if you search for "grocery store".

For other small needs, like band-aids or chocolate, you can purchase what you need at the serviced cabins and hotels.

If you want to purchase hiking gear while on the trail, take the bus to Lom or Vagå from the park and use one of the sporting goods stores there. If you have issues with your gear, many of the serviced cabins have fix-it kits that can be used to make minor gear repairs.

Timing

July through September are the best times to go. In June, Langsua will be clear, but there may still be quite a bit of snow in Jotunheimen. In October, the days are already starting to get shorter, and you may get heavy snowfall in Jotunheimen. Check SeNorge.no to see the latest snow report.

Camping

Norway has some of the most permissive laws in the world around camping. Norway has a law called the Allemannsretten that guarantees the ability of people to explore and experience nature, even in privately owned areas, as long as you're in uncultivated land. Once you're in the wilderness, you may camp in any area, as long as you're at least 150 meters away from the nearest inhabited house or cabin.

Note that the 150 meters applies to the DNT cabins as well - most serviced cabins have marked areas where you can camp, and you'll have to pay a small fee to use the toilets or other common facilities.

Campfires are prohibited everywhere in Norway from April 15 to September 15, except in specifically marked areas in camping sites and by the coast. You will need to bring a gas stove to cook, and in the case of drought, even gas stoves may be banned.

Planning Resources

UT App and Checking In

You can check in on the UT app (which is sometimes referred to as "SjekkUT", or "check out") at the various cabins or landmarks that you stop at. The UT app only has instructions in Norwegian, so how to do that:

Following a hike – needs to be done in advance:

1. For starters, download the ut app. Once you've downloaded the app, make a profile with your email address and log in on your device.

2. From there, you have to follow the hikes that you want to take. Following the hikes will download the maps around the cabins or areas on that hike, so you'll be able to use them without internet service. This is important.

3. Adding the route to your account is not entirely intuitive. You will need to search for the name of the hike in the search bar. From here, the critical thing is that you follow the list, not the hike. It will be at the bottom of the search results.

4. Click on the list. Make sure it's the one with the list icon. If you click the three dots on the side, you'll get a button that says "Følge", or "follow." Click on that.

5. Congratulations! You have now followed the hike. The maps will download to your phone while you have service.

Checking in:

When you get to a cabin or landmark, you can check in. Click on the icon for the cabin or landmark on the map, and a little green button that says "SjekkUT" will show up on the bottom left. Click on it.

A new screen will pop up. Click on the green button at the bottom again. If you see a screen with confetti, you're checked in!

yr.no is the best resource for weather in Norway. It allows you to hike by specific cabin or mountaintop, with the weather for that particular point rather than the overall area. It's available in English.

Senorge.no shows the current and historic weather conditions for any point in Norway. It's very useful for checking the amount of snow remaining for summer hikes, as well as seeing if it's rained recently.

ut.no is an app and website with detailed maps of Norway with the cabins and trails marked. It's unfortunately only in Norwegian, but is the best source of information on cabins and trails. You can download offline maps by going to "Profil" and then "Mine offline-kart" on the app.

Varsom.no is key for the winter and shows storm and avalanche warnings. It's available in English.

If you're stopping by a DNT office before going hiking, you can pick up a planleggingskart, or planning map. These aren't usable for hiking but are great for planning, since they show the locations of cabins and DNT cabins.

The weather can be variable in Jotunheimen's peaks, so I recommend using YR to specifically look up the weather by cabin or mountaintop.

Packing List - Summer

In total, the gear below should weigh between 15 and 25 pounds (7 to 12 kilograms).

Gear

☐ **46-55 liter backpack** with a rain shield

☐ **Maps and compass:** the maps in this guide are overview maps, and I strongly recommend getting 1:50,000 hiking maps just in case you're caught out in low visibility conditions or your phone battery dies.

☐ **Hiking poles:** they were super useful for long, flatter sections, snowfields, and river fording for me. I also used them to poke the ground to make sure it was real ground and not just mud.

☐ **Duct tape:** for any small repairs underway.

☐ **Dry bags for packing:** I made the very expensive mistake of not wrapping my laptop in these. Don't make the same.

☐ **First aid kit**, particularly band-aids in case of blisters

Clothing

☐ **Hiking boots:** whether you use high or low hiking boots is up to you.

☐ **Trail runners:** these are optional, but I use mine to give my feet a break from heavy hiking boots, especially on flatter days.

☐ **Rain pants and optional gaiters:** in myr or grasses, the water from plants nearby will soak into your pants if you don't have rain pants or gaiters.

☐ **Rain jacket**

☐ **Windbreaker:** it's frequently misting in the mornings, so if you don't like hiking in your rain jacket, bring a lighter weight jacket to hike in.

☐ **Wool socks, two pairs:** I use one pair of socks for hiking and one pair for the cabin.

☐ **Hiking shorts (optional):** it may be warm enough to hike in shorts.

☐ **Hiking pants** or long underwear to layer under rain pants

☐ **Two sports bras and two pairs of underwear**

☐ **Wool sweater and extra warm jacket:** I wear this when I'm hiking in cooler conditions, and it's always helpful to have in case you

☐ **Hat and gloves**

☐ **Two hiking shirts:** I strongly recommend wool here - it won't get as smelly and will keep you warm even when it gets wet

Cabin Supplies

□ **Mini towel:** for cabins with showers. The showers are usually single gender but communal, so the towel is handy even if you want to create a little shield to get changed under.

□ **DNT key:** even if you're not planning to stay in the cabins, it's good to have in case of emergencies

□ **Sengetøy (sheet set)** or sleep liner: the blankets on the beds are not washed in between guests. You need to bring your own sheets to keep things clean

□ **Toilet shoes:** about half of the cabins have outdoor toilets, and this keeps you from having to put potentially wet hiking boots back on

□ **Sleep mask:** there are good curtains in the cabins, but it never gets dark

Food and Drink

□ **Thermos** for hot drinks

□ **Water bottle:** there are plenty of rivers and streams to fill up a water bottle as you're hiking

□ **Candy and snacks**

□ **Plastic bag for sandwiches**

Tech

□ **Phone:** I recommend downloading UT, YR, and Hyttebetaling before your hike

□ **Battery pack**

□ **Chargers:** many of the self-service cabins only have USB classic charging outlets. If you have a phone with a USB-C charging port, you will want to bring a USB to USB-C charger.

Other

□ **ID and credit cards:** there's no need to bring cash

□ **Sunglasses and sunscreen:** if it's sunny, you'll need sunscreen, particularly on the snowfields on Glittertinden and Galdhøpiggen

□ **Toiletries:** wilderness wash, face wash, toothpaste, toothbrush, contacts, contact lens solution, glasses, hairbrush, hair ties, nail clippers, any medications

□ **Tiny shovel and toilet paper**

□ **Extra plastic bags**

Packing List - Winter

What You're Wearing

There's a substantial amount of clothing and gear to wear on the ski trips - much more than on the summer trips:

☐ **Wool base layer, underwear, and socks**: I brought two pairs of socks for really cold days.

☐ **Wool sweater**: on still days, you can just wear this over your base layer to ski in.

☐ **Tights under your pants**: the best strategy is to use long underwear under ski pants. Make sure whatever layer this is is warm.

☐ **Hat, gloves, and neck buff**: I ended up wearing my hat even when I had the hood on my rain jacket up just for the extra warmth on my ears. I made sure my hat fit under my jacket hood.

☐ **Gaiters (optional)**: I passed a lot of people using gaiters, which made sure that snow couldn't get in the top of their ski boots.

☐ **Fjellskis, shoes, and poles**: fjellskis don't have a great translation in English, but they're wide skis with steel edges that can be used for ungroomed terrain. The boots are generally very large and robust - they look more like intense hiking boots than ski boots. If you are doing Jotunheimen's downhills on skis, you will also need a helmet.

☐ **55-70 liter hiking backpack** with a rain shield: if you're planning to camp, you might need something slightly bigger for food storage.

In your bag:

Additional clothing:

☐ **Extra set of clothes**: I took a full set of extra clothes (shirt, underwear, bra, leggings) with me. I wore it in the cabins and when I was letting my main set of clothes dry out.

☐ **Mittens**: gloves were good enough most days, but there were 2-3 days where I needed the super-warm mittens. If the weather forecast is substantially below zero, I'd also take hand warmers.

☐ **Cabin shoes**: inside the cabin, I just wore socks, but the trail runners kept my feet dry-ish on the walk to and from the outdoor bathrooms.

☐ **Down jacket or very thick sweater**: there were several days I ended up layering my top, sweater, down jacket, and then shell on top of it. I like the down jacket because it's light and easy to pack.

Gear:

☐ **Emergency bivvy (vindsekk):** It's essentially a giant waterproof and windproof bag that you can climb into, whether to eat lunch outside of the wind and snow, or if you need to spend the night outside

☐ **Sleeping bag:** in case you get stuck outside overnight,

☐ **Shovel:** for digging down into the snow when you stop for lunch or in case of avalanche. You may also need this if you get to a cabin and the door is blocked by snow - there is a shovel at the cabins, but it is sometimes under the snow.

☐ **Avalanche beacon** if you're going in steep terrain: make sure you know how to use it

☐ **First aid supplies:** I took a ton of bandaids on this trip and was happy that I did. I used an entire box. Otherwise, just the standard stuff here.

☐ **Toiletries:** don't take too much, and keep in mind there's very limited hot water.

☐ **Sitting pad:** for when you stop for lunch and need something to sit on.

☐ **Sunglasses and alpine ski goggles:** it's bright on the snow

☐ **Map and compass:** most of the trails are marked, but there are times where the sticks that mark the routes fall down or turn into reindeer snacks.

☐ **Thermos and plastic bag** for lunch: plastic bags to store sandwiches in, and the thermos to keep water from freezing. I filled my thermos with hot water every morning, and it was fantastic to drink it on the trail.

☐ **Ski wax or skins:** what you'll need depends on your exact skis .

☐ **Headlamp:** the days are short, so the headlamp is doubly important. It's also useful for going to the bathroom at night in the dark.

☐ **Duct tape and Swiss army knife:** in case you have any issues with your gear.

☐ **Snacks:** take some small snacks that you can put in your pockets or the side of your bag, since it's hard to stop and eat in the winters.

☐ **DNT key and membership card:** even if you're not planning to stay in a DNT cabin, take the key in case you need need to duck into a cabin for shelter

☐ **Battery pack** for phone and charger that works with USB outlet: the majority of the cabins have solar power and a USB plug for charging devices. Phone batteries can drain quickly in the cold, especially if you have an iPhone, so make sure to have a backup charger. The solar panels in the cabins can also be intermittent during the darkest season (January and February).

There isn't always service, so download the maps you need before you go.

Some Handy Norwegian Words

Almost all Norwegians speak perfect English. That said, there are times where it's handy to be able to read signs, the weather, or the map.

Hiking and the map

Bratt/meget bratt: steep/very steep

Breen: the glacier

Dalen: the valley

Grusvei: a gravel path

Luftig: steep drop offs on the side of the trail

Kvistet: marked (used for ski trails)

Merket: marked (used for summer trails)

Mobildekning: phone service

Myr: a swampy, wet land covering

Nord, sor, ost, vest: north, south, east, west

Skog: forest

Stein: rocky

Steinur: rocky patches to hike over

Tind/tinden: peak

Vadested: a place that requires wading

Vannet: the water

Varder: cairns

Vatnet: the lake

Vegen: the road

Weather

Bris: breeze

Flom: flood

Lettskyet: barely cloudy

Lyn: lighting

Nedbør: precipitation

Nysnø: new snow (no icy cover yet)

Regn: rain

Weather continued

Skyet: cloudy

Snø: snow

Sol: sun

Soloppgang, solnedgang: sunrise, sunset

Strynregen: very heavy rain

Tåkete: foggy

Torden: thunder

Things in provision rooms

Bønnemix: mixed beans

Erter: peas

Fullkorn: whole grain

Gryte: stew

Hermetikk: shelf-stable boxes

Kaffe: coffee

Kanel: cinnamon

Kokemalt: coffee that needs to be cooked in a kettle

Kjeks: biscuits

Kjøtt: meat

Knekkebrød: crispbread

Kokk uten lokk: cook without a lid

Kylling: chicken

Lapskaus: a Norwegian stew of potatoes and meat

Legg til: add to (e.g. "legg til vann" = "add water")

Linser: lentils

Melkepulver: milk powder (reconstitute with water)

Ost: cheese

Pannekake: pancakes

Food continued

Potetmos: mashed potatoes

Rein: reindeer

Ror godt: stir well

Smør: butter

Sodd: a high calorie stew of pork, potatoes, and some vegetables

Sukker: sugar

Svine: pork

Syltetøy: jam

Turmat: dehydrated hiking food

Vann: water

Cabins

Betjent: serviced (a lodge)

Selvbetjent: self-service (a cabin without staff but with a provision room)

Ubetjent: unserviced (a cabin with beds, propane, and wood, but no food)

Drikkevann: drinking water

Forhåndsbestilt: booked in advance

Hyttefelt: a collection of cabins

Protokoll: the book you have to sign when you arrive at a cabin

Using the Cabins

One of the most amazing things about hiking in Norway is the national cabin network. The Norwegian Trekking Association (DNT) maintains a network of more than 600 cabins spread across the country. It makes it easy to travel deep into the wilderness without carrying food or a tent.

Cabins come in three grades:

Betjent (serviced):

These aren't cabins but full lodges. You'll have a three course meal for dinner, a buffet breakfast with a place to fill your thermos, showers and drying rooms for clothes, and often indoor toilets.

Dinners are served family style, where the staff will bring out giant tureens of soup for a first course, then usually some kind of meat and potatoes, then individual desserts. There's more than enough food for everyone - but make sure to book ahead and alert the cabin if you have dietary restrictions.

The family style dinners mean that you have to go to an assigned dinner time, usually seven o'clock. There's usually assigned seating. People are generally super friendly at dinner and chat about where you've hiked from that day.

Serviced cabins have electricity, but the number of outlets varies. At many cabins, there are only outlets in the common areas. At others, the electricity is turned off after dinner service ends, so don't rely on an overnight charge for your devices.

Serviced cabins also have drying rooms and showers. Drying rooms usually have strong heaters and dehumidifiers that dry out gear overnight. Showers are usually communal for each gender, so if you're shy, try to go at an off-time.

You'll pack lunch for the next day at breakfast. There is parchment paper and sometimes plastic bags for taking sandwiches in - the Norwegians are generally happy to show you how to wrap a sandwich in parchment paper if you need help. The stay at an serviced cabin also includes a thermos fill up for the next morning - they'll let you know at check in if you should leave your thermos at the reception desk or bring it to breakfast to fill it up yourself.

Serviced cabins usually have a variety of room sizes, everything from 2 bed rooms to a dormitory room.

Selvbetjent (self-service)

Self-service cabins are unique to Norway. They're generally smaller than staffed cabins, but come fully stocked with a provisions room, wood for the fireplace, gas for cooking, and cooking supplies. Some have electricity, but it's usually from a single solar panel. You usually have to fetch and boil water from a nearby water source.

The self-service cabins run on the honor system. They can be unlocked with the DNT key, which you can purchase at a DNT store in Norway, online at their web store ahead of the hike, or at a staffed cabin. To pay for your stay, use the Hyttebetaling app. The app allows you to keep a list of all the supplies you've used and then pay with credit card when you get back into phone service. The app is available in English.

Ubetjent (unserviced)

These are just like self-service cabins, except that there isn't food available in the provision room. There are no ubetjent cabins on Omveien.

Cabin Etiquette:

When you arrive at an unserviced or self-service cabin, the first thing to do is to unlock the cabin and then take off your shoes. No outdoor shoes are allowed in the cabin to help keep it clean. After that, fill in your information in the besøksprotokoll, a horizontal blue book that asks where you came from, where you're going, and your membership information. After that, you have the right to use the cabin. I generally first start a fire if the cabin is cold, then fetch water to heat up for dinner.

When you leave the cabin in the morning, you'll need to clean up. That means washing all of the dishes, cleaning out the ashes in the fireplace, bringing in fresh wood for the fire, washing the floors in the bedroom and common areas, and any other tidying.

You can use the cabins if you're camping. You'll need to register in the besøksprotokoll and pay for a day visit ("dagsbesøk"). After that, you can cook food or just relax for a bit. Make sure to sweep up and wash the floor after yourself.

Cabin FAQs:

It's not necessary to book in advance for the cabins - if you arrive at the cabin, you'll have a place to sleep, though it might be on a mattress on the floor if it's really busy. I generally don't book cabins in advance so that I have the most flexibility possible to change hiking plans based on the weather.

Book ahead at the serviced cabins if you have dietary restrictions. Because meals are served family style, the cabins need advance notice to be able to accommodate dietary restrictions.

Most of the cabins in Langsua close during the spring for reindeer breeding season. Otherwise, self-serviced and unserviced cabins are generally open year round. UT.no will have information on cabin opening times.

Joining DNT:

You should absolutely join DNT - the savings on staying in the cabin will cover the cost of the membership in two to three nights. If you are planning to camp, you will still want to join DNT to get a DNT key. You'll need the key if you want to do a day visit or if you end up staying in a cabin during a day with particularly bad weather.

Joining online is a little confusing, and there are updated instructions on the blog. You can also stop by any DNT office in Norway.

Cooking at the cabin:

There is a propane stove and plenty of cooking supplies in the cabins. The food that you'll generally find breaks down into four categories:

Breakfast: knekkebrød , oatmeal mixes, pancake mix, leverposti (liver spread), jam and chocolate spread, mackerel in tomatoes, butter, jam, and honey

Dinner: fish soup, peas and carrots, mashed potato mix, lapskaus, rice, bacalo, boxed mixes for Pasta di Parma and Chili Con Carne, pasta, reindeer meatballs, dry red lentils, and crushed tomatoes

Snacks and dessert: chocolate pudding, vanilla sauce, canned fruit in syrup, and biscuits

Misc things: dried hiking food, coffee, tea, hot chocolate, currant drink mix, hiking snacks like knekkebrød sandwiches, sugar, cinnamon

My challenge with cooking at self-service cabins is finding something to bring for lunch the next day. I really load up on breakfast, often mixing vanilla sauce or jam into my oatmeal for the extra calories. I take two or three packages of freeze dried food with me to eat on the trail, in case there isn't shelf-stable cheese and knekkebrød for lunch.

Each cabin has a different selection of food, and if you're late in the season, certain items might be eaten up. If you're vegetarian or gluten-free, make sure to have your own backup food

Omveien FAQs

Can I drink the water underway? Do I need to bring a water filter?
You can drink water directly from streams in Norway, and you'll see the Norwegians doing just that. The cabins also have places where you can fill up water bottles, so no need to bring a water filter. Use common sense - don't drink the water where there are clearly sheep grazing.

Where can I leave luggage?
If you have luggage or items that you don't want to bring on the hike, the best place to leave them is at the Oslo airport or train station, or in the Lillehammer train station. Officially, the luggage lockers can only be used for seven days, but it's often possible to leave items for longer as well. Email hittegods.osl@no.issworld.com for the airport or oppbevaring@banenor.no for the train station, and let them know your locker number and plans.

What about luggage transport?
Sorry, you're out of luckYou'll need to carry everything that you want to bring with you on the trip. Pack lightly.

Can you section hike the trail?
Yes! It's easiest to split it into Langsua and Jotunheimen, using Gjendesheim as the break point, but you can also pick any two cabins with public transit links (see the "How to Get There" section) and just do that section.

Am I okay just speaking English?
Absolutely. In my entire time in Norway, I have met only three people who couldn't speak English. Jotunheimen especially has lots of foreign guests. The only challenge is that the labels on food in the self-service cabins are only in Norwegian. I've included some key words in the book for reading food labels.

Is it expensive?
It's about $100/night to stay in a serviced cabin, which includes all food, and $30/night to stay in a self-service cabin. It's a lot cheaper than other hiking trips I've taken because you don't have to pay for a hotel room - you pay by person rather than room. If you want to save on the cost, you can camp some nights rather than staying in the cabins.

Can I do laundry along the way?
You can handwash clothes at the cabins and then dry them in the drying room or over the fire, but that's it. There are no laundry facilities.

Can I rely on the self-service cabins to have food and supplies?
Yes - I've visited 121 DNT cabins so far and have yet to find one that wasn't stocked. If you have dietary restrictions, though, make sure to bring some backup food. It can get a little boring on day 3 or 4 - I recommend bringing a few small things to spice up your meals.

How hard is navigation?
It's not bad at all - the trails are generally really well marked with the characteristic red T and very visible cairns. I used my phone rather than a map and compass. The UT app was a huge help.

That being said, I took maps and compass in case my phone died – that turned out to be a good move, because I broke my phone after falling through a snow bridge at the end of the hike.

Will I have phone service?
I've listed which cabins have phone service in the cabin amenity section, but generally, you should expect to have phone service for most of the hike. Leirvassbu, Spiterstulen, and Gjendesheim even have wifi. Phone service generally varies during the course of the day - even if two cabins both have phone service, the hike in between them may not.

Are there bugs?
Unfortunately, yes in a few spots. I didn't have any in Langsua, but I had a relatively dry period. Around Leirvassbu was the worst.

When can I go?
July through September are the best times to go. In June, Langsua will be clear, but there may still be quite a bit of snow in Jotunheimen. In October, the days are already starting to get shorter, and you may get heavy snowfall in Jotunheimen. Check SeNorge.no to see the latest snow report.

What's the biggest mistake people make with this hike?
Overpacking. You'll need to have clothes that are warm enough for going over Glittertinden in Jotunheimen, but you'll also need clothes that you can wear on warm days in the sun. Don't bring extras, though. There's no need for cute clothes in any of the cabins. Also, make sure you have waterproof shoes for the beginning of Langsua, and in the snow in Jotunheimen.

Can I do this in the winter?
Yes! It's possible to do Omveien on skis, with two modifications - you'll need to turn south from Oskampen and ski to Bygdin, then over to Gjendesheim from Bygdin. You cannot go over Sikkilsdalsseter directly because of avalanche-prone terrain. You'll also need to go from Skogadalsbøen to Fondsbu to end the trip, as Vettismorki is in avalanche prone terrain as well.

That being said, it's a tough route to do during the winter. The areas in Langsua are easy on fjellski, or Norwegian backcountry skis, but Jotunheimen requires good knowledge of how to go down steep slopes and general fitness.

Cabin Overview

Cabin that evening	Cabin Type	Beds	Pre-bookable beds	Power	
Skjellbreidhytta	Self-service	7	4	Y - 12 volt (USB)	
Kittilbua	Self-service	7	3	Y - 220 volt	
Vestfjellhytta	Self-service	18	10	Y - 12 volt (USB)	
Liomseter	Serviced	51	51	Y - 220 volt	
Fehytta	Self-service	10	5	Y - 12 volt (USB)	
Storkvolvbua	Self-service	27	9	Y - 12 volt (USB)	
Storhøliseter	Self-service	18	10	Y - 12 volt (USB)	
Oskampen	Self-service	12	4	Y - 12 volt (USB)	
Sikkilsdalsseter	Serviced, private	78	78	Y - 220 volt	
Gjendesheim	Serviced	185	185	Y - 220 volt	
Glitterheim	Serviced	137	137	Y - 220 volt	
Spiterstulen	Serviced, private	280	280	Y - 220 volt	
Leirvassbu	Serviced	205	205	Y - 220 volt	
Olavsbu	Self-service	52	25	Y - 12 volt (USB)	
Skogadalsbøen	Serviced	87	87	Y - 220 volt	
Vettismorki	Self-service	9	5	Y - 12 volt (USB)	

Phone Service	Drying Room	Shower	Drop point?	Other Notes
N	N	N	No	
Y	N	N	No	
Y - termittent	N	N	No	
N	Y	Y	Yes - limited bus service	Bus service only during peak season
N	N	N	No	Only open when Liomseter is closed. Small and basic cabin
	N	N	No	
Y - termittent	N	N	No	
N	N	N	No	
Y	Y	Y	No	Connects Jotunheimen to Langsua national park
Y	Y	Y	Yes - buses to Lom, Oslo, and others	
N	Y	Y	No	Nearest bus stop is Randsverk, 7 km from the cabin on a road
Y	Y	Y	Yes - bus service to Lom	
Y	Y	Y	Yes - bus service to Lom	Very large, modern cabin - even has wifi
N	N	N	No	
N	Y	Y	No	Phone service near the stone building about 100 meters from the cabin
Y - termittent	N	N	No	

Sarah Rowe has solo hiked more than 4,500 kilometers across 24 countries, with a focus on Norway and Austria. She's the recipient of DNT's golden key, having visited more than 100 DNT cabins, and has hiked seven of DNT's thirteen SignaTUR tours.

When she's not out hiking, she's writing about it on her blog, Solo Female Wanderer, drinking coffee, and planning the next adventure.

Questions or comments? You can reach her at
sarah@solofemalewanderer.com